How to Win
Your Family
to Christ

How to Win Your Family to Christ

by Nathanael Olson

GOOD NEWS PUBLISHERS
Westchester, Illinois 60153

How to Win Your Family to Christ
Revised edition, Copyright © 1977
by Good News Publishers, Westchester, Illinois 60153
First edition published in 1961.
More than 240,000 copies now in print.

Library of Congress Catalog Card Number 77-81561
ISBN 0-89107-149-0

Contents

Introduction
Does God Will the Salvation of Your Entire Family?

Introduction

Both the Old Testament and the New Testament pulsate with the truth that God is willing and able to save the believer's entire family.

God said to Noah, "Come thou and *all thy house* into the ark, for thee have I seen righteous before me in this generation" (Genesis 7:1, emphasis added).

Before the night of the Passover, God laid down the principle of "a lamb *for a house*" (Exodus 12:3, emphasis added).

Rahab, listed in God's Hall of Faith (Hebrews 11), believed for the protection of *all her family* during the destruction of Jericho. Her petition was granted. She and her family were unharmed (Joshua 2:12-21; 6:25).

Paul and Silas told the Philippian jailer, "Believe on the Lord Jesus Christ and thou shalt be

saved *and thy house*" (Acts 16:31, emphasis
added).

Cornelius was promised that Simon Peter "shall
tell thee words, whereby thou and *all thy house*
shall be saved" (Acts 11:14, emphasis added).

There are many other Scripture verses which
give assurance that God desires to bring each family member into the Ark of Safety. (See Proverbs
11:21; Psalm 103:17; 1 Corinthians 7:14.)

The Apostle Peter reminds us that the Lord
is *"not* willing that any should perish but that
all should come to repentance" (II Peter 3:9,
emphasis added). He wants to save your mate,
your parents, your children, and all other members of your family circle. And He wants to work
through you in bringing about this thrilling miracle.

"All my family saved?" you gasp; "that seems
an impossibility." But Jesus says, "... with God all
things are possible" (Mark 10:27). If you are with
God and God is with you, nothing is impossible!
When Martha had difficulty comprehending how
the Lord could bring her brother, Lazarus, back to
life, Jesus said, "... if thou wouldst believe, thou
should see the glory of God" (John 11:40).

Spiritual men and women through the ages
have claimed their families for Christ, and God
has honored their faith. Catherine Booth of the
Salvation Army exclaimed, "Oh, God, I will not
stand before Thee without my family!" Her entire
family came to know Christ and served Him faithfully. Jonathan Edwards claimed his descendants
for the Lord, and a thorough investigation has

shown each descendant has made a profession of faith in Christ.

Dr. Theodore H. Epp of the Back to the Bible radio ministry writes: "The salvation of a believer's family is a precious truth revealed in the Holy Scriptures."

The late Dr. Harry Ironside, for years pastor of Moody Memorial Church, said, "It is the desire of God to save the household of His people."

Dr. Donald Grey Barnhouse stated: "It was after an evening spent with Jesus that Andrew went to find Simon Peter. If you are seeking the salvation of loved ones, spend more time with the Savior."

Concerning *family* soul-winning, famed London pastor Charles Spurgeon wrote:

"Though grace does not run in the blood, and regeneration is not of blood nor birth, yet doth it very frequently—I was about to say almost always—happen that God, by means of one of a household, draws the rest to Himself. He calls an individual, and then uses him to be a sort of spiritual decoy to bring the rest of the family into the Gospel net."

"God has not reversed the laws of nature, but He has sanctified them by the rules of grace; it augurs nothing of selfishness that a man should seek to have his own kindred saved. I will give nothing for your love for the wide world, if you have not a special love for your own household. The rule of Paul may, with a little variation, be applied here; we are to 'do good to all men, but especially to such as be of the household of faith';

so we are to seek the good of all mankind, but specially of those who are of our own near kindred. Let Abraham's prayer be for Ishmael, let Hannah pray for Samuel, let Andrew first find his own brother Simon, and Eunice train her Timothy; they will be nonetheless large and prevalent in their pleadings for others, because they were mindful of those allied to them by ties of blood."

In the following pages, you will discover guidelines to help you do the right things and avoid the wrong things in bringing your family to Christ. This counsel has helped a quarter of a million readers since this book was first published. May this new and revised edition help *you* to win *your* family to Christ!

If I can be of further help, do not hesitate to write to me in care of Familytime Ministries, Post Office Box 400, Milwaukee, Wisconsin 53201.

Yours to unite families for time and eternity,

                                        Nathanael Olson

Chapter One

Your Husband Can Be Won

Chapter One

Mrs. J. of California knows that a husband can be won to Christ. It took 24 years of praying, trials, and consistent Christian living. Her husband is a happy, Christian businessman today.

Here is the letter she wrote the author.

It took 24 years to win my husband. It was a long, thorn-crowned path that I walked but I never gave up. Even when things looked the blackest, I would reason: "Well, even if my husband never gets converted, I will still try to do my part by the grace of God."

Each day I tried to please Jesus. Many times I went through very hard places. I was at death's door several times. My children often suffered from serious illnesses. I can remember days, during the depression, when we didn't have one dime to buy food. The power company cut off our electricity. I washed by hand for our four small children. When we'd get a few dollars, my husband would spend them for liquor. In desperation, I would pray and ask God to miraculously supply food for my little ones. And God heard me. We never starved. Of course, my children couldn't figure out where Mama got the food. It was a secret between the Lord and me.

My husband was a hard-headed Swede. He knew he should become a Christian. He told me that he knew Christ had changed my life when I was converted. He admitted that God had done miracles for our family. But he would not pay the price of being an out-and-out Christian father.

He seemed to go in cycles. Sometimes he didn't want religion discussed; other times he seemed hungry for reality. During these latter times, I would witness to him about Christ. At other times, he would become very angry if I mentioned the Lord. But when I couldn't talk to him about God, I would talk to God about him. He couldn't stop me from praying for him.

It wasn't long until I became aware that my husband was being unfaithful to me and to his marriage vows. Of course, he tried to hide this fact from me. But one day, while I was praying, God seemed to show me where my husband was, and who he was having an affair with. My heart was broken. Naturally, my husband denied the whole matter. But I found out later that God had shown me the tragic truth. My husband was unfaithful.

God enabled me to keep a Christian disposition through these dark hours. I tried never to aggravate him. When he was in a bad mood and made cutting remarks, I kept quiet. Each day I found a new supply of patience, endurance, and closeness in the Lord. I certainly didn't have any of these qualities when I came to the Lord. I had too much of my natural Irish in me, I guess. Before my conversion, I was stubborn, quick-tempered, and saucy. But then, I allowed Jesus to take over my life. And He changed me completely. In fact, other Christians told me that I was "too easy going," that I should defend myself. But God told me to keep sweet and let the Lord defend me.

In 1950, our home and our business were really going on the rocks. I was tempted to tell my hubby that he could do his own praying from now on. (I knew that he seemed to feel a certain amount of security from my prayers.)

But then, as someone has said, "the darkest hour of the night is just before the dawn." After 24 long years of tears, heartaches, prayers, and persistence, I saw my husband go to the altar in an evangelistic meeting. The prodigal husband had come home to God at last. I was bubbling over with joy.

Today, after many years, my husband is still serving the Lord. We have a Christian home, go to church together, and run a successful business.

If God could perform a miracle in our home, He can do it in any home. With the Lord's help, I know a woman can win her husband to Christ!

Multiplied thousands of husbands have been won to Christ by their dedicated wives. But remember, these women didn't do some things which they realized would drive their husbands away from the Lord. Other things they did do which they knew would attract them to the Savior. Like any successful salesman, these wives followed definite steps toward making the sale.

Take the true story of Mrs. J. She didn't tell her husband church troubles (which many a wife has foolishly done when he is just looking for more excuses to stay away from church). She didn't

argue with him; she didn't threaten divorce. She
didn't feed him religion from morning to night.
But she did witness to him when he was "in the
mood" for reality. Mrs. J. kept on praying and
believing. She kept a Christian disposition, and
she refused to accept defeat. Finally, she took him
to church where he met Christ as his personal
Saviour. At last, her "do's and don'ts" paid off.

Let's consider a few positives and negatives
which will help you to win that "man of mine" to
Christ.

1. Don't Nag or Preach at Him

If anything will drive your husband from Christ
it is this feminine trait, nagging. You must get
the victory over it. I know you mean well. You
want to see him improve. But nagging is trying to
do a right thing in a wrong way. This negative
trait will produce only negative results. Instead,
praise him for his good points, and say sweetly,
"I'm praying that God will help you with those
other areas...."

Preaching at your husband will make him feel
that you have a "holier than thou" attitude. Jesus
didn't say that He would make you a preacher. But
He did say that He would give you a supernatural
power to be a witness, one who has something
worthwhile to say when given the opportunity.

Mrs. H. remembers, with regret, what her
preaching did to her husband. As a new convert,
full of joy and zeal, she tried to force Christianity
on her unbelieving husband. But her preaching

only drove him farther from the Lord, and from his "gift of the gab" wife. One day he left her!

Remember, all your words will be hollow and meaningless, unless the Holy Spirit has prepared your husband's heart for the Gospel seed. So pray more and preach less. Ten words backed with the power of God will do more in ten seconds than a thousand words given in your own strength will do in ten years.

2. Don't Tell Too Much in Your Prayer Requests

Many a well-meaning, burdened wife tells too much of family troubles in her prayer requests. She uses too many adjectives and descriptive phrases in making the need known. "My husband is so grouchy that I can hardly live with him. Please pray for him. He still smokes and swears. He sure needs God's help, etc."

As a result, many husbands won't go to church. "My wife has told them what an awful sinner I am. I feel self-conscious in that church. They know all my faults...."

Please, forget the symptoms of sin, and just deal with the root of the trouble. Say, "I need your prayers that I may win my unsaved husband to Christ."

If you must tell your troubles to someone, confide in your pastor. But never tell your tale of woe to a whole congregation.

3. Don't Compare Him With Other Husbands

Here's an example: Mrs. B. to Mr. B. "I wish

you'd take me to church like Mr. F. takes his wife. He even takes their children to Sunday School. I wish you were like he is...."

It's so easy to fall into this comparison rut. But please stay out of it. Your comparisons will only injure your husband's pride. Instead, make him feel that he's the best husband in the world (oh yes, he has his faults, but so has every other husband). If you must compare him, compare him with himself. For instance, tell him that he's a good husband and provider but that you feel the children would think that he's even greater if he'd go to Sunday School with them. This appeals to his natural desire for self-improvement. Try it. It works!

4. Don't Make His Habits the Big Issue

Remember, the reason he sins is because he is a sinner. Until he accepts Christ, he is powerless to overcome these habits. Therefore, your big concern should be his receiving Christ, not his dropping habits.

If you pick on his habits, he will find a few of yours to pick on too. An unsaved husband in Wisconsin confessed: "Sure, I smoke and drink, but my Christian wife gossips and gets mad. I have two bad habits and she has two, so we're equal."

Have you total victory over your disposition, temper, and tongue? If not, you had better not talk much about your husband's habits. Just talk about his receiving or rejecting Christ. After all, his habits won't send him to hell. Only his unbelief will. Therefore, help him with his biggest sin, unbelief.

A woman said to D. L. Moody: "Please pray for my unsaved husband. He does many bad things, but he has a good heart."

"That's where you're wrong, lady," the great evangelist answered. "He does bad things because he has a bad heart. Out of the heart are the issues of life. He needs a new heart."

That's what your husband needs, Christian wife. He needs a new heart. And when God gives him new desires, "he will hate the things he once loved, and love the things he once hated." So deal with his heart. The habits will look after themselves.

5. Don't Compromise

Never compromise your standards and beliefs in the hope that if you are not "too strict," perhaps you will win your husband. Firmly, but kindly, take your stand and your husband will respect you for it.

The famous newscaster, Paul Harvey, tells of an uncertain soldier in the Civil War, who, figuring to play it safe, dressed himself in a blue coat and gray trousers and tip-toed out into the field of battle. What happened? He got shot at from both directions! Compromise didn't help him.

Nor did it help a Christian wife who decided to please her husband by "just once" attending a dance with him. For years, she has refused to go to dances with him. But it seemingly hadn't helped her to win him to Christ. Therefore, she decided to give in. Perhaps if she would be broad-minded one time, he might go to church with her all the time. So she went with him to the dance and was his partner for the evening.

"Thank you, honey, for a very enjoyable evening," he smiled, as they walked into their living room. She beamed at him.

"Now I'm sure you'll go to church with me this Sunday," she said. "Won't you?"

His smile turned to a frown. "I certainly won't," he snapped. "I thought you had reality in this Christian faith, but after tonight, I know this faith must not be very strong if you could give in to my request." Then he added thoughtfully, "I made up my mind that if you had refused to go with me this time, I would know that you had something real. I would have gone to church with you to find out for myself. But now I know that it's just a fad, not a strong faith...."

Don't learn the compromise lesson the hard way. God says, "... The way of transgressors is hard" (Proverbs 13:15). Compromise is a transgression and the results are always tragic. So keep true to God, His Word, and your faith. Your faithfulness will convince your husband that what you have is genuine.

We have considered five important "don'ts." Now let's look at a few vital "do's" in winning your husband to Christ.

1. Live the Life—the Christian Life

A Chinese man said that he had never heard the Gospel of Christ but that he had seen the Gospel in the life of a woman in the village nearby.

Remember, seeing is believing. Your husband will never believe the Gospel he hears until he believes the Gospel he sees—in you. If he sees that God has given you control over your temper, tongue, and attitudes, he likely will trust the Lord for victory over his ungodly habits, too.

The hardest part of Christianity is living the life. Going to church, teaching a Sunday school class, attending prayer meeting, reading your Bible is easy compared with the acid test of your faith, living the life. It has been said that "Christianity has never been tried and found wanting, but it has been tried and found difficult and therefore abandoned."

Here's what Dr. Oswald J. Smith says:

Don't argue. Quarreling raises the blood pressure. Submit ... Live peaceably (Romans 12:18). Nothing separates like argument. Give in, even if you know you are right. Don't be stubborn or dogmatic. Learn to yield. Better to remain silent than to antagonize. Argument creates feeling, and feeling temper. It may not be easy, but it is possible. Practice restraint. Take it to the Lord in prayer. If you feel that you are never wrong and if you can never apologize and say "I'm sorry," if you are always ready to argue the point, you will be certain to grieve the Holy Spirit and you will never be perfectly united in love. There will be an ugly chasm between. Therefore, if you want to be happy, don't argue. God's grace is always sufficient. Never forget that the husband is the head; he is the head to carry out his wife's plans as queen of the home.

2. Love Him to Christ

A sinner is not preached up, argued up, or forced up from the pit of sin. He must be loved up. This is why a woman holds the biggest key in winning a man to Christ. Your love or lack of love can be the deciding factor in your husband's decision about Christ.

Just recently, a minister was counseling with the father of four children. This man had come to the altar for salvation. He said that smoking and drinking were the least of his troubles. "It's my home life," he sighed. "If my Christian wife and I could get things straightened out, I know I could really serve the Lord."

Perhaps you feel that you love your husband enough. But do you show it? Martha loved Jesus but Mary showed her love. "Men are won by Marys, not by Marthas. All the Marthas in the world could never win a man's heart. It is Mary who wins...." So says Dr. Oswald J. Smith. He further admonishes wives to: "... go to him with open arms. Take time to express your love. Give him an opportunity to enjoy your affection. Go to him often. Make love to him even if he is old. Be so indispensable that he will never even think of anyone else."

Christian wife, never measure your love with that shown by your neighbor. Rather, examine your love in the light of 1 Corinthians 13. See if you show this type of love to your husband. Also read the last chapter of Proverbs for tips on how to be more than "just a housewife."

3. *Appeal For His Help in Rearing the Children–Religiously*

This is one of the very strongest appeals—that of being a good father. No man wants to be a "flop as a pop." Therefore, convince your husband that Bible reading in a family fashion will help solve the problems of your family. Urge him, for the children's sake, to attend Sunday school and church with you. Tell him that little Johnny says he wants to grow up to be "just like Dad." Then ask your husband to set a good example for Johnny by attending church, at least on Sunday mornings. See if this doesn't appeal to his ego. Many a husband has been won to Christ through this approach.

One of the greatest thought-provokers to show fathers that being a good provider is not enough is Dr. Joplin's famous version of the Prodigal Son. He calls it: "The Prodigal Father." I suggest that you write or type a copy of this sobering story, and get your husband to read it when he's in the right mood.

A certain man had two sons and the younger of them said to his father, "Father give me the portion of thy time, and thy attention, and thy companionship, and thy counsel and guidance which falleth to me." And he divided unto him his living, in that he paid his boy's bills and sent him to a select preparatory school and to dancing schools and to college, and tried to believe that he was doing his full duty by his son.

And not many days after, the father gathered all his interests and aspirations and ambitions and took his journeys into a far country, into a land of stocks and bonds and securities and other things which do not interest a boy, and there he wasted his precious opportunity of being a chum to his son. And when he had spent the very best of his life and had gained money, but had failed to find any satisfaction, there arose a mighty famine in his heart, and he began to be in want of sympathy and real companionship.

And he went and joined himself to one of the clubs of that country and they elected him chairman of the House Committee, and president of the club, and sent him to the legislature. And he fain would have satisfied himself with the husks that other men did eat, and no man gave him any real friendship.

But when he came to himself, he said: "How many of my acquaintance have boys whom they understand and who understand them, who talk about their boys and associate with their boys and seem perfectly happy in the comradeship of their sons, and I perish here with heart hunger? I will arise and go to my son and will say unto him: 'Son, I have sinned against heaven and in thy sight and am no more worthy to be called thy father. Make me as one of thy acquaintances.' " And he arose and came to his son.

But while he was yet afar off, his son saw him and was moved with astonishment, and instead of running and falling on his neck, he drew back and was ill at ease. And the father said unto him, "Son, I have sinned against heaven and in thy sight. I have not been a father to you, and I am no more worthy to be called thy father. Forgive me now, and let me be your chum."

But the son said: "Not so, for it is too late. There was a time when I wanted your companionship and advice and counsel, but you were too busy. I got the information and the companionship, but I got the wrong kind, and now, alas, I am wrecked in soul and body. It is too late—too late—too late!"

4. *Discover Your Husband's Area of Response*

Before David killed Goliath, he had discovered the one weak spot in the giant's armor. And before you can win your husband to Christ, you must discover his greatest area of response, his hidden interest. In plain language, it is the inward desire of a person. For example, every true Christian wants to be a soul-winner. Most women want to look pretty; most men want to be successful. These are our hidden desires.

Your husband may want to be a more successful businessman. Well, get him a book about the millionaire industrialist, R. G. LeTourneau. He will discover LeTourneau's success: "taking God as my partner."

Perhaps he's always wanted to be a singer. Then take him to hear Bev Shea, Doug Oldham, or a host of other sacred vocalists. Or maybe he likes music but not preaching. Treat him to a sacred concert.

Does he love to eat? Then take him to a church supper that has a Gospel program following the meal. Many men are attracted to the banquets and programs of the Christian Business Men's Committee.

If sports are his great love, take him to hear one of the well-known sports personalities from the Fellowship of Christian Athletes.

Learn to take an interest in the things he likes, and you will discover that he will take more of an interest in what you like. Marriage is a two-way street.

It is reported that Evangelist D. L. Moody played tennis with a young man so that he could win his confidence. After several hours of good, clean sport, Moody led him to Christ.

Don't be afraid to try some different bait in fishing for the soul of your husband. Perhaps one of the above suggestions may be the bait that will make your husband "taste and see that the Lord is good." We sincerely hope so.

5. *Learn How to Work Through Others*

Winning your husband to Christ is a big job. You may need the help of other Christians. But you must inspire them to help you tactfully reach your husband's soul.

F. W. Woolworth said: "Our company never really expanded until I realized through a nervous breakdown that I couldn't do everything myself. So I learned to work through others and our business boomed."

Billy Graham recently stated that he did not think that he had ever really won a soul to Christ single-handedly. He feels that he is just a link in a chain of people and events that bring a soul to Christ.

Christian wife, you are the most vital link in this chain. But still you need the help of others.

First, you need the prayer support of other believers. Make sure your husband's name is on the prayer list of several of your friends.

Second, you need the help of Christian men. Remember, men understand men.

A good Christian man can help change your husband's attitudes toward Christ, by showing him that a Christian man can be happy, successful, and a good sport. Perhaps you can urge Mr. X to become friends with your husband. You feel that their common interest, fishing, will make them "buddies." And you're likely right. Many a sinner has been convinced that Christianity is up-to-date by seeing Christian men having fun on a fishing trip.

So try to get your husband a friend who will be a "man's man" and "God's man" at the same time.

Third, work through your children. Details are given in another chapter.

The Bible says: "Use all means to win some." This includes working through others: prayer groups, Christian men, your children.

Dr. J. C. Brumfield has some vital thoughts on the subject of winning your husband to Christ. Through the kind permission of Back to the Bible Publishers of Lincoln, Nebraska, we freely share with you excerpts from his excellent booklet on this subject. His remarks are based on a portion of scripture: I Peter 3:1-6, which reads:

Likewise, ye wives, be in subjection to your own husbands; that, if any obey not the word, they also may without the word be won by the conversation of the wives; while they behold your chaste conversation coupled with fear. Whose adorning let it not be outward adorning of plaiting the hair, and of wearing of gold, or of putting on of apparel; But let it be the hidden man of the heart, in that which is not corruptible, even the ornament of a meek and quiet spirit, which is in the sight of God of great price. For after this manner in the old time the holy women also, who trusted in God, adorned themselves, being in subjection unto their own husbands.

Dr. Brumfield makes these suggestions:

Let us take some words out of the first verse of this passage as our text—"they may be won." Speaking to Christian wives concerning their unsaved husbands, God says, "They may be won." What a wonderful promise!

The wife can win her husband to the Lord if she meets the conditions which God has set forth in His Word. He does not promise that the preacher can win him, or that friends can win him (and surely God uses these instruments sometimes); but He promises that the wife can win him. He gives directions affecting three things: attitude, appearance, and adornment. They have to do with the Spirit, the body, and the soul.

The wife's attitude must be that of loving, reverential submission to her husband. This is according to God's Word, not an invention or theory of mine.

Notice these words in the first verse: "Likewise, ye wives, be in subjection to your own husbands." This is a direct reference to I Peter 2:18 where the servants are asked to be subject to their master. Wives are to practice this same obedience with their husbands. "Likewise" also refers the reader to the second part of verse 18, where Peter acknowledges that some masters are cruel or "froward," but calls for obedience to them as well.

The application to the home is that if a woman finds herself married to an ungodly or even a cruel husband, she is to bear her suffering just as Christ did, trusting God to take care of the injustice suffered. Her obligation before God, who originated the marriage institution, is to be obedient.

I have the utmost sympathy for the woman who has to live with an ungodly man. Her love has been betrayed, her romance has faded, her dreams have vanished, her hopes are shattered, and her heart is broken. If this is your situation, my purpose is to help you claim God's promise and win your husband to the Savior. To do this, I must speak frankly; and some things that I am going to say may hurt. If you will accept these suggestions as from the Lord, you will some day rejoice in a home made happy in Christ.

There are several reasons for subjection. You will find some of them in the following references: I Corinthians 11:8-10; I Timothy 2:11-14; Ephesians 5:23, 30.

God requires you to be in subjection to your own husband, not to some stranger. In the Word of God every time a woman is commanded to *obey* her husband, a Greek word meaning, "one's own dear husband" is used. An altogether different word is used for *husband* alone.

Be in subjection to "your own dear husband." That is not unreasonable, is it? Of all the men in the world you chose him to be your life companion, to share sorrow and happiness, to be the father of your children, to be the protector of your home, and to be the provider of your needs. You chose to have a more intimate relationship with him than with anybody else on earth. You left father and mother (incidentally, you were in subjection to them when you were with them) to live with him in preference to all other men.

If you will follow God's instructions, you can win your husband back to your heart and also to the Lord. You will never accomplish anything toward winning your husband to Christ, however, until you are willing to follow God's plan. The very first step is loving, trust-

ing, sacred, holy submission to the man of all men,
"your own dear husband." God says that this is the only
basis upon which a happy home can be founded. It is
the only way in which an unsaved husband can be won
to Christ.

To what extent should the wife obey her husband? I
cannot agree with some very good Bible scholars who
say that a wife should obey her husband even if it
means that she must engage in sin, stay away from
church, never read God's Word, never pray, never listen to Gospel broadcasts, and never have Christian fellowship.

God has given us some plain commandments regard-
ing sin, and certainly they do not justify anything like
that. Notice what He says in Romans 6:13: "Neither
yield ye your members as instruments of unrighteousness unto sin." That is God's commandment, and it
affects your relationship to every other person in the
world. God says that you should not yield your members as instruments unto sin, but "yield yourselves
unto God." You should first be yielded unto God.
"Submit yourselves therefore to God" (James 4:7).

If there is a conflict in your mind as to whether you
should obey God or your husband, you should remember Acts 5:29: "We ought to obey God rather than
men."

God gives a wonderful promise to the faithful, loving,
submissive Christian wife: "They may be won." In the
oldest manuscripts that word *may* is stronger; it literally means "shall"—an almost objective certainty. God
is saying that if you carry out His directions, your husband "shall be won."

The word *conversation* does not mean "much talking." God says, "They may be won by the behavior of
the wife." Some people would say that the Word is the
only thing that God can use to bring about regener-

ation. That is right, but the Word can be lived in a life sometimes more powerfully than it can be spoken with the lips. That is what God is promising here. The husband may be won by the behavior of the wife in the home and in the family relations. What a challenge to Christian wives! Directly from God himself comes the promise—"won by your behavior, by your manner of living, by your conduct." God actually makes the Christian wife responsible for the salvation of her husband.

A nagging, irritable, complaining, careless, unpleasant woman will never win her unsaved husband to Christ. You say, "Any woman would be cross and irritable if she had to live with the kind of man I have." You will have to continue to live with that kind of man until you yourself become a little sweeter. Your behavior in the home has more to do with your winning your husband to Christ than all the sermons he might hear. You preach to him that Jesus can free him from his sins, help him overcome drinking, swearing, and the use of tobacco; but unless you show him that Jesus can cure that temper of yours, control your tongue, and sweeten your disposition, your words will have little effect on him.

God says in the second verse, "They behold your chaste conversation coupled with fear." In other words, they will observe your pure, spotless behavior, coupled with reverential fear toward them, and "they may be won."

How will your husband be won? Through your life! When your manner of living is changed and you have godly fear and love for your husband, God will use you to win your husband to the Lord.

You may make excuses for your past behavior and for your failure to obey God's command, but I want to tell you again that God's Word tells every Christian wife that her unsaved husband may be won; not by hearing Gospel sermons, because he may not listen to a sermon; not by going to church, because he may not attend God's house; not by reading the Bible, because he may never read the Bible; not by sacred Christian companionship, because he does not have friends like that. The only contact that most unsaved husbands have with Christians is with their wives in the home. God declares that they may be won by the "conversation (the manner of living, the behavior) of the wives."

How does it work? Look again at that verse. "They behold your chaste conversation (behavior) coupled with fear." If you are a Christian wife with an unsaved husband, will you not pray, "God, teach me from Thy Word how I might be used as an instrument in Thy hands to win the one whom I love to Christ."

The second condition has to do with the wife's appearance. "Whose adorning let it not be that outward adorning of plaiting the hair, and of wearing of gold, or of putting on of apparel." Some have interpreted this verse as meaning that a Christian woman should not arrange her hair becomingly, wear jewelry, or be attractive in her personal appearance. If that is what God is teaching here, the same interpretation must be applied to the last part of that verse, "or putting on of apparel." In that case, she should not wear clothing. Common sense tells us that God does not mean that.

Nowhere does God condemn a Christian wife for being clean, neat, and attractive. Some women would make more progress in winning their husbands to Christ if they gave a little attention to their personal appearance. I suggest very kindly that if some women would spend about ten minutes looking in the mirror, they might discover why their husbands do not make love to them any longer. A man spends the day in the business or professional world, where he sees women who are neat and well-groomed. Then he comes home at night to find his wife looking like a "washed sheet in the breeze." There seems to be a connection between cleanliness and godliness which some Christian women have not discovered. Perhaps you have become negligent in regard to some of these very important things.

God teaches us that the Christian woman should not cheapen her appearance by gaudy ornaments and worldly attire in order to attract attention. But nowhere does He condemn a woman for making the best of her personal appearance in order to hold the love and admiration of her husband.

But mere outer adorning is not the only way to win your husband to Christ. There is a real adornment, however, that will reach his heart. Notice the fourth verse. "Let it be the hidden man of the heart." The literal translation of this is the "regenerated heart adorned by the Spirit of God." This adornment "is not corruptible"; it is not tainted, as is all earthly adornment.

Notice the last part of this verse: "Even the ornament of a meek and quiet spirit." He is saying that the adornment that will attract your husband to Christ is not that of jewelry, fancy hairdress, etc., but the inner adorning of the heart—the adornment of a meek and quiet spirit.

A meek spirit is one which does not create a disturbance, which is not officious and "bossy." A quiet spirit is one which bears with patience the disturbance caused by others and is gentle in word and action.

Now notice the fifth verse. "After this manner (a meek, quiet spirit) in the old time the holy women also, who trusted in God, adorned themselves, being in subjection unto their own husbands." That adornment, in other words, was not the outer adorning which we have mentioned, but the wife's subordination and "a meek and quiet spirit."

God is saying that what has worked in the past will work for you. The subjection of these women did not consist of slavery, but the inner adorning of the heart, which is a Christ-like spirit.

How can you win your husband to Christ? In the first place, by loving, reverential subjection. He is your own husband, the man whom you married. Perhaps by your insubordination you have literally broken your marriage vows. You will never get anywhere that way. Be meek, sweet, kind, gentle, patient, submissive, and loving. Never be loud, frivolous or giddy. Ask God to give you grace in this matter.

Be careful that your desire to win your husband to Christ is prompted by the proper motive—the glory of God. Many sincere Christian wives have failed in this respect. The want their husbands saved so that their lives will be happier and their homes more peaceful. Because they have a selfish motive, God has not answered their prayers. Ask God to give you a concern for the soul of your husband, that whatever it may cost you in sacrifice or suffering, his soul might be saved for the Lord's glory.

When your husband comes home this evening, meet him with a smile. Have your hair combed neatly and have a clean, becoming dress on. Try to look just like you used to when he came to take you out for a date. Be sure that the house is spick-and-span and homey-looking. Have an appetizing meal on the table; serve his favorite dish. Be sweet, kind, cheerful, softspoken, and submissive to your husband. He may faint; but when he recovers, he will like it. If you continue to act in this way, according to God's promises, your husband will be won to the Lord.

To encourage you in your thrilling but difficult task of winning your husband to Christ, we conclude this chapter with one of the most heart-touching conversion stories of our times: The First Mate Bob story, which he calls "Eight Bells." It is used through the kind permission of First Mate Bob himself, Paul Myers. It is written by his wife.

Things were always happening at our house. I used to tell the family that we ought to write a book and call it, *Never a Dull Moment*. We would answer the telephone, above the children's hearty din, with 'Grand Central Station!'

It would be impossible to put down on these too few pages anything but a bare outline of that story, and this I will try to do; but first I must say that as I look back over the years of my marriage and especially as I dwell on the years since I began loving and serving my Savior, one thought, one conviction shines through it all; it is that the undergirding of the Everlasting Arms, the love of God shed abroad in hearts, the protection and covering of the precious blood are absolute essentials for living a happy, serene, useful life. This is the message of my story and my reason for writing it.

One of my earliest girlhood memories is of my mother's going to work to support my younger brother and me. When I was ten, I worked too, during the summer and winter vacations. Coming from a home that was broken by divorce, I craved love and affection, and so I spent a good deal of time with my aunts, who loved me and who brought the first spiritual influence into my life—one of them gave me my first Bible.

I remember a Sunday morning when I was thirteen; I went to the altar, and later that year I was baptized. It was a definite step of faith, yet somehow I wasn't satisfied. I read my Bible, but did not understand it at all. I faithfully went to Sunday school and church, where most of the lessons and sermons were of Moses, Elijah, and the prophets; nothing of the marvelous, matchless, free gift of grace of the loving Son of God which I was later so gloriously to know. These were years of spiritual seeking and years of growing, physically at least, for with them I left girlhood behind.

I remember when I met Paul. I was sixteen and he was—well—wonderful, if I may say so. We fell deeply in love and about two years later were married. That was December 16, 1920, and in that marriage I gained not only a dear husband, but also a lovely little girl, for Paul had a little daughter, Marilyn, whose mother, his first wife, had died soon after the child's birth.

Paul's mother was a dear, sweet Christian; she took me into her heart and into her family with Paul's five sisters (all younger than he) who, down through the years, have counted me as one of them. His parents and oldest sister have long since been called home to Glory, but their Christian lives made a deep impression on me and were a big influence in my life.

Two years after our marriage, God sent us another little girl, Patricia Ruth; and when she was nine months old, both she and little Marilyn contracted very severe cases of whooping cough. It was at this trying time that Satan chose to strike at our marriage—I became aware that my husband was unfaithful. Night after night with two very sick little girls I was left alone. I was desperate!

Those were indeed dark days. My mother, seeking to help me, took me to church. There, for the first time, I heard about Jesus who loved me and gave himself for me that I might have everlasting life. I learned that all that was required of me was an open heart to receive and an obedient will. I went to the altar, with hundreds of others, and received Christ as my Savior. On July 24, 1924, I was really born again, a definite "know-so" experience. (God also touched my daughters' bodies and made them well.)

For ten long years I prayed for my husband's salvation. Many times the skies seemed as brass, but I had faith in the promises of Acts 16:31: "Believe on the Lord Jesus Christ and thou shalt be saved, AND THY HOUSE." Still there were many lessons in grace that I needed to learn, so I read and marked my Bible and spent many nights on my face before the Lord. My Bible still shows where the tears fell. I knew the Lord had a plan for my life; my one desire was to walk in His will and way. When asked why I didn't leave my husband, my only answer was to quote I Corinthians 7:10-16, "Let not the wife depart from her husband: ... For the unbelieving husband is sanctified by the wife, and the unbelieving wife is sanctified by the husband: else were your children unclean; but now are they holy."

The Lord sent us two more lovely children, Peggy June and our only son, Richard Eugene. I took them to Sunday school and taught them to pray. The responsibility of raising and training four children would have been too much but for His wisdom and the knowledge of His promise of Hebrews 13:5. He promised never to leave me alone. I claimed the blood for a household; by faith I applied the blood of God's Lamb to the doorposts of my home. One by one each of the children received Christ as his personal Savior. Only my husband was out of the fold.

In the matter of disciplining the children, the Word of God is very plain; so when there was deliberate disobedience in any case, I read to them from the Word, then applied the psychology of "laying on of hands" in the proper places. The pancake turner was usually the handiest instrument. If a child learns obedience in the home, it is easier for him to be obedient to the laws of the land and much easier to be an obedient child to his heavenly Father. Even Jesus had to learn obedience (Hebrews 5:7-9). Oh yes, here are some of the Scriptures I used: "Train up a child in the way he should go: and when he is old, he will not depart from it" (Proverbs 22:6). "Foolishness is bound in the heart of a child; but the rod of correction shall drive it far from him" (Proverbs 22:15). "Withhold not correction from the child: for if thou beatest him with the rod, he shall not die. Thou shalt beat him with the rod, and shalt deliver his soul from hell" (Proverbs 23:13-14). "The rod and reproof give wisdom: but a child left to himself bringeth his mother to shame" (Proverbs 29:15). And Samuel said, "Hath the Lord as great delight in burnt offerings and sacrifices, as in obeying the voice of the Lord? Behold, to obey is better than sacrifice, and to hearken than the fat of rams" (1 Samuel 15:22).

There came a time in each child's life when, through sickness or accident, I realized that they were only a charge given me for a while. As I would kneel by their beds when they were ill and the decision had to be made, I would say, "Yes, Lord, she is Yours. If it is Your will to take her to Yourself, I can say, 'Amen.'" Arriving at that place of decision was not easy, but oh the joy and peace of knowing positively that He watched over each child, day and night, even when I could not be with them.

When Dickie was five years old he became desperately ill, and there came the time of decision again. I did not know where my husband was, and although he had been gone for months, God had provided for our every need. He had promised and I believed that ... "my God shall supply all your need according to His riches in Glory by Christ Jesus" (Philippians 4:19). Dickie had a fever of 105 degrees for hours, and there was no money for a doctor. I knelt by his little bed and prayed far into the night.

It was indeed a dark night, but for a mother who had a living God to pray to and a burning faith to light her every way, the darkness seemed only to shut out the world and make more clear the gleaming path of prayer that led to the throne of God's abiding grace.

She prayed on. And as she prayed, God looked down on a hopeless, desolate figure of a man as he groped his way aimlessly through the wintry darkness of a distant, slumbering city.

The last, deep blackness of night enshrouded the wharves and warehouses of the San Diego waterfront. There was little or no activity to be seen. Occasionally a darting taxi would flash into view only to disappear around the corner of a deserted street. Against a foggy sky, the riding lights of the harbored craft moved in monotonous rhythm with the rise and fall of the restless water. Intermittently, the weirdly protesting groans of the hulls of vessels chafing against their moorings could be heard. Chill fingers of mist began to settle down here and there, and the man, Paul Myers, looking back on that fateful night, recalls:

As far as I could see, I was alone, not another human being was in sight as on and on I trudged.

Long hours before, I had begun this aimless wandering and now weary in body and mind and sick of soul, I still was as bewildered and lost as ever. Memories, like haunting ghosts of all the dead yesterdays, followed my every footstep. The faces of my wife and four children kept appearing again and again upon the screen of my consciousness. How were they tonight? I had left them alone and helpless! Here was I, a wanderer and a derelict! Wave after wave of awful self-condemnation swept my very soul.

A nearby piling offered a seat, that I might rest my aching feet. The cardboard I had put in my shoes to protect my feet where the soles were worn through had long since ceased to serve its purpose.

Only the lapping of water against the wharf broke the stillness of the night. The sudden clanging of a ship's bell startled me. Two ... four ... six ... eight— eight bells ... "that must be four o'clock in the morning." I had walked all night in an alcoholic stupor, for I had been drinking heavily, trying to forget.

Shivering the cold I sat there and, like the sudden changing of a screen drama, a trick of memory carried me back across the years to an old-fashioned family altar where once I knelt and prayed. Many years had passed since we laid our mother to rest down by the western sea, but it seemed as though I could hear again the sound of her voice as she taught me to sing the old songs of Jesus and His love, and to lisp the words of life from God's holy Book. Echoes of all-but-forgotten old hymns came drifting out of the distant past.

How vividly now I recalled the many times my sweet Christian wife had pleaded with me to accept as my personal Savior the Lord Jesus Christ she knew and loved so well. Her prayers and those of my children had followed me, I knew. All the years of my life, my proud heart had rebelled against a full and complete surrender. I had gone my own willful way; and to a marked degree, I had been successful in a business way. I had become well known in radio circles, and finally had been appointed to an important position as an executive manager of two radio stations in Southern

California. Now all this was a thing of the past, and I was fact to face with the dead-end street of life at "eight bells in the morning watch!"

Eight bells! That was the end of the long night watch and soon it would be morning. Morning to me meant just another dreary day. All at once it dawned upon me that this morning would be Sunday morning. The people of San Diego would be gathering for Sunday school and church. Church! How long had it been since I had sat in a church and heard a sermon and joined in worship? So long I couldn't remember. I used to sing in a choir long ago. Perhaps, if I could find someone who would pray with me, there would come some peace to my troubled heart and soul. That was it! I needed God! I remembered mother's oft-told tale of the prodigal son. If ever there was a prodigal son, it was I!

Never shall I forget that Sunday morning in 1934. My last few pennies went for a frugal breakfast. A convenient gasoline station washroom afforded the means of making myself as presentable as possible. Long before the appointed time for the morning service I entered the open door of a large church whose bell had heralded the morning worship up and down the streets of the city. Here at last I would find Christian men and women who would stretch forth a friendly hand, who would help me find my way back. Eagerly I sat and listened to the organ, the choir and the preliminary rituals. The pews were well filled with well-dressed men and women who had come to listen to the Word of God. At last the minister began his sermon.

It was all over. The benediction had been pronounced, the choir had sung its last amen and people were slowly filing out. No one had spoken a word to me. No mention had been made in the morning message of a Savior who could rescue a lost soul. The whole meeting had been so coldly formalistic that I had not de-

tected one single smile. No hand of greeting had been
extended to me. True, I needed a shave, my clothes
were shabby and I was disheveled and unkempt; but
surely, I thought, that would make no difference to
Christian men and women. I was stunned!

I found my way back to the cheap room where I had
been sleeping, and I expected to be refused admittance,
for I already owed a week's rent, but I made it. I was
desperate! Suddenly my eyes were focused upon a book.
It was a Gideon Bible, placed there by that great band
of Christian businessmen known the world over. I had
carelessly noticed its presence before, but now it
seemed to hold out to me a faint ray of hope. Opening
its pages I placed it upon a chair and knelt before it. I
do not recall reading a single word. I simply began to
pour out my heart to God, acknowledging my guilt as a
sinner and declaring my faith in Jesus Christ to save
my soul.

Then and there I passed from death unto life. I became a new creature in Christ Jesus. An indescribably
wonderful peace settled down upon my soul. The load
was lifted, my weight of sin rolled away and the "light
of the knowledge of the glory of God" burst in upon my
sin-sick, sin-cursed soul. I had found that "joy un-
speakable and full of glory" which is the sweetness of
the indwelling presence of the Christ of God. I tried to
sing but I could not for my voice was completely gone.
For almost a year and a half my voice had been just a
husky whisper. But prayer and praise do not come from
a human voice, they come from the heart, and God
looks at the heart. "Oh God," I prayed, "if You'll only
straighten out my life I'll serve You all the rest of my
days." God began to work that very moment in my life.

Would my wife take me back? I wouldn't blame her if
she wouldn't. I'd go back to Los Angeles and see. Car-
fare home? I didn't have a penny; I'd have to hitchhike

my way. I didn't know how God was going to work it all out, but I had the absolute assurance that whatever came in my life would be best for me and it was well with my soul. I would give my best effort to my Lord and the rest was up to Him. So, at last I came back home to my wife and kiddies.

"Thelma, I have found Christ, and He's real to me at last." This was my greeting to her who was the mother of my babies. God alone knows how many sleepless nights she prayed for my soul's salvation. With the wonderful love of Christ in her heart she took me back. (Christ is not only the healer of broken lives and broken hearts, but the healer of broken homes, as well! How often since that day have I seen Him bring together estranged husband and wife in the sweet bonds of fellowship.)

"Honey," I said, "I am going into full-time service for the Lord. I don't know where or how, but I made Him that promise, and I know He'll open up a door somewhere." She prayed with me that God would have His way.

Radio was the only thing I knew. I had spent years before a microphone in commercial broadcasts of all kinds. That was it: a broadcast of gospel hymns and short evangelistic messages. I couldn't preach, but I could tell others of what God had done for me. But I had almost no voice at all. Nevertheless, God kept speaking to my heart, "Radio is where I'd have you." "All right, Lord," I prayed, "You tell me where to go and whom to see. Open the door, and I'll do my best." Thus began the ministry which today is known to the listening public as the "Haven of Rest."

The God who answered Thelma Myer's prayers will answer yours too. You can win your husband to Christ! Why not start in earnest—NOW?

Chapter Two
Your Children
Can Be Won

Chapter Two

The following accounts of the fate of two families reveal some shocking contrasts:

Max Jukes lived in the state of New York. He did not believe in Christian training. He married a girl of like character. From this union they have studied 1,026 descendants. Three hundred of them died prematurely. One hundred were sent to the penitentiary for an average of 13 years each. One hundred and ninety were public prostitutes. There were 100 drunkards, and the family cost the state $1,200,000. They made no contribution to society.

Jonathan Edwards lived in the same state. He believed in Christian training. He married a girl of like character. From this union they have studied 729 descendants. Out of this family have come 300 preachers, 65 college professors, 13 university presidents, 60 authors of good books, three United States congressmen, and one vice-president of the United States; and outside of Aaron Burr, a grandson of Edwards, who married a questionable character, the family has not cost the state a single dollar. The difference in two families: Christian training in youth and heart conversions.

A poet said:

> Some children walk the high road
> While others tread the low;
> A mother can determine
> Which way her child will go.

The Bible says, in no uncertain tone: "Train up a child in the way he should go, and when he is old he will not depart from it" (Proverbs 22:6). What is your responsibility? Train him. God's promise is that He will keep him on the right road.

Roger Babson, nationally known businessman and author says: "There's 1,000 times the temptation we had 25 years ago for our children today."

"Our children are fighting their greatest battle of our times.... Youth are being exploited by forces of evil on every hand and juvenile delinquency is rising.... Crime, Communism, atheism, immoral and evil influences are all working overtime, trying to tear down our wholesome family life."

But there is a bright side to this picture. The Bible says: "... Where sin abounded, grace did much more abound" (Romans 5:20). Yes, God has more saving grace for your family than the devil has temptations and sin. He will enable you to win your children to Him who said: "Suffer the little children to come unto Me, and forbid them not, for of such is the kingdom of God" (Mark 10:4).

Your children are your responsibility. As one mother expressed it: "When God gives us those precious pink and blue bundles of joy, He entrusts us with souls who are worth more to Him than all the world. We dare not fail Him or them. We must not allow these precious souls to be lost."

What a potential there is in that life of your child. Someone has clothed this fact with these beautiful words: "When a boy or girl thrusts his small hand in yours, it may be smeared with chocolate ice cream, or grimy from petting a dog, and there may be a wart under the right thumb and a bandage around the little finger.

"But the most important thing about his hands is that they are the hands of the future. These are hands that someday may hold a Bible or a Colt revolver; play the church piano, or spin a gambling wheel; gently dress a leper's wound, or tremble wretchedly uncontrolled by an alcoholic mind.

"Right now, that hand is yours. It asks for help and guidance. It represents a full-fledged personality in miniature to be respected as a separate individual whose day-to-day growth into Christian adulthood is your responsibility."

Guide that hand to Christ by following these time-tested guideposts to successful, Christian training:

1. The Family Altar

This point is right where it should be—at the top of the list! The family altar is of paramount importance in child-training. Church or Sunday

school can never take its place. Why? Well, one
good reason is the time element. Did you know,
according to the John Rudin Company of Chicago,
that of the 105,000 waking hours from childhood
to maturity, only 1,000 hours are spent in Sunday
school; only 7,000 hours are spent in public school,
but 97,000 hours are spent in the home? Percent-
age wise, that means less than one per cent of
those hours are spent in Sunday school; only
seven per cent in school, and 92 per cent at home.
Why not give religious training where the children spend most of their time—in the home?

Remember, "A family altar would alter many a
family." And it still is true that "the family that
prays together stays together." We cannot leave
all the teaching and training to a 45-minute
period on Sunday morning no more than we would
leave all our eating for a Sunday dinner!

"Yours is a delinquent family if you do not
counsel, pray, and study, and worship together,"
warns V. E. Fridley. "If these activities are mis-
sing in your home, you are rearing potential
juvenile delinquents. If this happens, it will not be
the fault of the children. The responsibility will be
on you."

How do you find time for a Family Altar? You
don't. You *take* time. You snatch a half hour of
your day to watch your favorite television program, or 15 minutes to read the newspaper, because you want to. And if you really want to have
family devotions, you will take time from something else that isn't so important. Your motto will
be, "No Bible—no breakfast!"

Mrs. Susanah Wesley, mother of 19 children, *took* one hour out every afternoon for prayer. And she lived in a day when mothers made their children's clothes and often had to be the teachers of their children. No automatic washing machine, no diaper service, no grocery delivery, yet she spent a "sweet hour of prayer" every day. No wonder two of her sons became the great revivalists, John and Charles Wesley!

Remember, if you're too busy to pray, you're just too busy. And your life, your family will suffer from "the barrenness of busyness."

Therefore, decide upon a definite time, either morning or evening, when the whole family can be together, if only for five or six minutes. Stick to this time in spite of any possible interruptions. Let nothing keep you and your family away from this rendezvous with the Lord.

How can you, as a Christian parent, keep this family altar time from getting monotonous for your children? Well, you can vary your Bible reading—such as adventure stories one week: David and Goliath, the walls of Jericho, Gideon and his 300 men; love stories the next week: Isaac and Rebecca, Mary and Joseph, and so on.

Children love contests. Why not give a prize to your child for learning a memory verse each day or each week?

Scripture hunts add zest to Bible reading. Perhaps each Saturday, see which one of your children can find the verse the quickest. Use your concordance, and call out several references on one theme: obedience, reverence, honesty, or whatever is the current problem in the family.

If you have a Bible with colorful pictures of the Holy Land or reproductions of famous religious masterpieces, tie them in with your Bible reading. We are living in a picture-loving age. Therefore, use pictures to spark interest in the greatest Book ever written. A picture is worth 10,000 words.

Vary your prayer time. It can be either a form or a force. The way you handle it will make the difference.

Don't do all the praying yourself. Teach each child to pray in his or her own way. It may be just a sentence prayer. But one sentence from your child's heart is better than eight sentences of "canned" prayer. As soon as possible, break your children from the habit of just saying memorized prayers. You will find that they love prayer time better if they can say their own "home-made" prayers. Give them sincere praise when they pray well.

If your children are old enough to read, prayer requests may be written on slips of paper and put in a prayer-request hat. Each member of the family takes out one, two, or three requests from the hat. This adds the element of surprise which children love.

Praying for missionaries and learning geography can be tied together easily by this plan. Cut out a map of Africa, India, South America, and other mission fields, and paste the name of the missionary on the part of the country he or she is ministering in. In this way, your child will visualize a country as he prays. "Dear God, bless

Missionary Jones in Nigeria as he tries to help those lepers get better and find Jesus," is a sample of what we mean by geographical, visualized praying.

The Lord will help you develop your own ideas to keep the family altar fresh, interest-packed, and a spiritual powerhouse for the kingdom of God in your home and around the world.

Who should lead in the family altar? Preferably, the father. If he leads the home in finances and discipline, he should also lead in the forming of Christian character, without which nothing else really matters.

Unfortunately, too many modern fathers have the attitude of the husband to the Shunamite woman as recorded in Second Kings, chapter four. When their son became ill and needed and cried for his father's help, the father said to a lad nearby, "Carry him to his mother." Many a man today has echoed this father's excuse: "Carry our children to their mother for religious training. I'm too busy making a living."

How wonderful it is when a father does realize and accept his responsibility. Mr. Wesley L. Gustafson had such a father. He remembers: "My father always had a family altar, in the morning and in the evening. As soon as the meal was over in the evening, he would get out the family Bible and read it. And in the morning, even when we had much work to do in the field and would have to be out early, he would get us up early enough to spend time with Christ before we would go to our work. Now he sees the results in his children's

Christian homes."

But if a father shirks his God-given task,
Mother must come to the rescue. Many a saint
says: "I learned about God at my mother's knee."

Strickland Gillilan says:

> You may have tangible wealth untold,
> Caskets of jewels and coffers of gold;
> But richer than I you will never be
> For I had a mother who read to me.

If you don't have a family altar in your home, by
all means begin one now. Remember, "the longer
you wait, the steeper the grade ... tomorrow may
be too late!" Parent, "their future is in the hollow
of your hand."

But you ask: "If I start a family altar, can I be
sure that it will bring my children to Christ? Will
it do a miracle in our home?"

We believe it will. Listen to what four au-
thorities say:

"When I was ministering to the men in an Ar-
kansas penitentiary," says Chaplain Hogg, "out of
1,700 convicts I found only one who had been
brought up in a home where they had an old-
fashioned family altar. I have heard since that he
was pardoned, as he was found innocent of the
crime with which he was charged. There is an
atmosphere in the Christian home which makes it
impossible for skepticism or atheism to live there.
May God give us back the old-fashioned family
altar, and the old-fashioned Bible, and old-
fashioned parents!"

The late Dr. Walter Wilson used to say, "Take

the book of Proverbs, and in it you will find 31 chapters, one for each day of the month. For one year, read a chapter a day, and I will promise on the basis of personal experience, the professional background of 40 years as a practicing physician, and yet more years as a Christian, that *every* problem of youth will be found and met in that one book."

"Remember the Word of God: 'Train up a child in the way that he should go, and when he is old, he will not depart from it" (Proverbs 22:6). This promise to other generations is for us to claim today. God will bring unto Himself those who have had proper training. This is an absolute fact. But we can't let the training go and claim the promise. If I want my children to know God, I have to train them. Then I can trust His promise—He will take care of bringing each of them to himself."—Wesley L. Gustafson.

"If they have the background of a godly, happy home and this unshakable faith that the Bible is indeed the Word of God, they will have a foundation that the forces of hell cannot shake."—Ruth Bell Graham.

So do your part, parent. Train your child at home by erecting a family altar now. That's the first, the greatest step in leading your children to Christ. Don't let this opportunity slip through your fingers. God will require an answer some day. What will you tell Him?

2. *The Sunday School*

Ralph Miller hits the nail on the head with

these truth-packed words: "*Sending* your children to Sunday school will certainly help. *Taking* them is better. *Taking them with you* is best...."

Why the emphasis on Sunday school as the second guidepost to family soul-winning?

Because "eighty-two per cent of the church world came out of Sunday school classes."

Because William James, the great psychologist said, "A person rarely ever changes his habits after he as reached his majority years."

Because Judge Fawcett, of Brooklyn, New York, said that out of 2,700 boys brought before his court, not one of them was a Sunday school pupil.

Because former President Woodrow Wilson stated: "There can be no liberal education without a knowledge of the Bible." The Sunday school teaches the Bible. It is the official textbook.

Three reasons, plus scores of others could be given why we feel that the Sunday school is a "must" in winning your children to Christ. And only real illness or some other definite emergency should be allowed to keep you or your children away from the most wonderful hour of the week—the Sunday school hour. No extra "40 winks" or a car ride to Aunt Susie's or Grandpa's can take the place of what the Sunday school does for your family.

Are you a parent who says, "I do not want my child to get too much church. I want my child to decide for himself about religion." Do you let your child decide if he should be honest or dishonest, truthful or untruthful, if he will go to church or stay at home? Do you let your small child decide for himself if it is safe to play with matches? Does he skip a day of school each week so he will not get tired of it? If you don't let him make these decisions, why let him decide the important matter of religion?

If the Sunday school near you is what it should be, your children will have teachers who are soul-winners. In fact, where you fail, they may succeed. Therefore, pray that the Lord will use Johnny's Sunday school teacher to help lead Johnny to Christ. Remember, it was a godly Sunday school teacher named Edward Kimball who won D. L. Moody to Christ.

A close relative to the Sunday school is the Vacation Bible School, which has the characteristics of an adult evangelistic campaign but has the appeal that children love: handwork, contests, and learning with fun. The VBS is one of the greatest modern day soul-winners. It may win your children to Christ.

Add variety to your child's spiritual diet by allowing him to attend summer youth camps, Bible clubs, Youth for Christ rallies. If he's an up-and-coming Einstein, Moody Science films will fascinate him and give him the Gospel in a delightfully-different way.

And what about Christian reading for Christian living? Do you encourage your children to read from the vast library of excellent Christian children's books available today at reasonable prices? Charles A. Wells said, "The school will teach children *how* to read, but the environment of the

home must teach them *what* to read. The school
can teach them how to *think,* but the home must
teach them what to *believe.*"

Why not win your children to Christ through
Christian comic books or Christian red-blooded
adventure stories such as the fascinating Narnia
series by C. S. Lewis.

The Apostle Paul told Timothy: "Give atten-
dance to reading." What your children read is
what they will become. Therefore, use the powerful printed page to lead your children to the Lord.

But remember this: Christian books, Sunday
school classes and even family altar will fail unless you include this essential element:

3. *Living a Consistent, Christian Life*

Someone asked a small boy: "Are your parents
Christians?"

"Oh, I guess they are," he drawled, "but they
aren't working very hard at it!"

No one can see through people like a child. And
your children are judging Christianity by the way
they see Mother and Father live it.

India's Ghandi said, "I'd become a Christian if it
weren't for the Christians I know."

On the other hand, there is Bob M., a Christian
young man who can truthfully say, "I have never
seen my parents argue before me."

And there is the man, who when others were
discussing the King James, American Standard,
and other versions of the Bible, declared: "The
best version of the Bible is the one my mother
lived!"

Quarles, the great writer, tells how the only thing that kept him from becoming an infidel was the one argument in favor of Christianity: the consistent, Christ character and example of his father.

Example is still the best teacher. Meditate on these following gems of thought:

You can preach a better sermon with your life than with your lips.

We can do more good by being good than in any other way.—*Rowland Hill*.

A Father who whipped his son for swearing and swore himself whilst he whipped him, did more harm by his example than good by his correction.—*Fuller*

Example is the school of mankind; they will learn at no other.—*Beecher*.

Such as is thy behavior before thy children's faces, such is theirs behind thy back.—*Quarles*.

There is a transcendent power in example. We reform others unconsciously when we walk upright.—*Switchine*.

None preaches better than the ant and she says nothing.—*Franklin*.

Parents wonder why the streams are bitter when they themselves have poisoned the fountain.—*Locke*.

Parents who wish to train up their children in the way they should go, must go in the way which they would have their children go.

When Plato saw a child do mischief, he corrected the child's father for the wrong.

You ask, "Well, what kind of an example should I be in order to show my children that Christianity is real?" The Bible has the answer in Galatians,

the fifth chapter, verse 22: "... The fruit of the
Spirit is love, joy, peace, longsuffering, gentleness,
goodness, faith, meekness, temperance...." If you
will show these qualities every hour of every day,
your children will know that you've "been with
Jesus." The light from your life will show them
the way to Jesus.

Closely related to living the life is our next point
in leading your children to Christ:

4. Firm Discipline Given in Love

"Spare the rod and spoil the child" is a time-
tested saying. The Bible says, "The rod and reproof give wisdom, but a child left to himself
bringeth his mother to shame." "Correct thy son,
and he shall give thee rest; yea, he shall give delight unto thy soul" (Proverbs 29:15, 17).

We are living in a day of self-expression, thanks
to our easing up on the reins of discipline. Has it
paid off? Are children and youth happier now that
Father is nothing but the "old man" and Mother is
the "old lady?" The newspaper headlines give the
sickening answer: "Eighty Teen-Age Girls Disappear in Last Month" ... "Police Capture Gang of
Car Thieves, All Under 16" ... "Sex Crimes Among
Juveniles On the Increase."

Parents who do not give firm discipline, tem-
pered with love, are hurting themselves and their
children. We need a revival of parental fear. If
your child does not respect you (fear you) he will
not love you.

One thing is certain: parents must be agreed on

the necessity of discipline. Divided parents cause confused children. So agree on what discipline is best: a heart-to-heart talk, taking away some privileges, or "the board of education on the seat of understanding." Agree on one or the other—and stick to it!

You ask, "Why will discipline help me to lead my children to Christ?" Here are some reasons:

a. Correction is taught in the Bible. God knew that mankind is strong-willed in the wrong direction. That will must be curbed, must be redirected into constructive channels. And you as a parent must begin that process.

b. Discipline is a vital part of the Christian life. The Bible says that "the Lord loveth whom he chasteneth." The Apostle Paul said he "must keep under his body." How can an adult master these Christian essentials unless his mother or father has taught him the value of discipline while he was a child?

c. Reverential fear precedes salvation. The Bible says: "The fear of the Lord is the beginning of wisdom ..." (Psalm 111:10). You can never expect your child to fear God and his commandments until he or she learns to reverence you and your word. In fact, your child's ideas of God are in direct proportion to his ideas of you. If you are an ever-loving, never-punishing parent, how will he believe that a God of love can and *does* punish Christ-rejecting souls in an eternal hell?

Give discipline in a loving but firm manner. If you lose your temper, or apply punishment mercilessly, you need "the licking" more than the child. But if you punish your child with a broken heart and a strong hand, God will smile His approval on you. He will use it as a step in leading your child to Him.

Another important step in family soul-winning is:

5. *Meet Your Child's Psychological Needs*

"Dad was always too busy for family fun or going on fishing trips with me." "I never felt that I could confide in Mother. I was afraid she wouldn't understand my personal problems." These are common complaints of the younger generation. They say they don't "feel close" to their parents.

This statement is tragically true. Many find, Christian parents lose their children right at this point because they don't meet the needs of their children's particular personalities.

For example: do you tell your children "the facts of life" in a sensible, unembarrassed Christian manner? I have found only one Christian young man who could proudly say: "Yes, my Christian father told me what I should know about life and love." All the others agreed: "Our fathers were cowards. They wouldn't discuss the subject, as if it were something sinful. So we learned it in the back alleys and from smutty pictures and books."

And far too few Christian mothers tell their daughters about the sanctity of sex. Are mothers ashamed of God's beautiful plan of reproduction?

And then Christian parents wonder why they lose their children to the wrong crowd. The reason should be obvious. They have found others who have the same problems, who understand them, and who listen when they talk to them.

The parents of Christian teenagers are not having as much influence on their children as one would suppose, according to a recent survey released by *Youth for Christ* magazine.

Less than ten per cent of the young people questioned said that their decision to become Christians was made through parental influence. Most of them gave "friends" or the "sermon" as the key factors.

Less than half say they can discuss their personal problems with their parents, and more than two-thirds prefer to go to their friends with their problems. In answer to the question, "Why didn't you become a Christian sooner?" thirty-seven per cent said they were not given the opportunity, and seventeen per cent replied, "I thought I already was a Christian." Only thirteen per cent gave "fear and pride" as the reasons.

Parent, determine now to make your child know that he or she can tell you anything, any problem, any plan, and that you will understand. The closer that soul feels to you, the closer he will come to God.

Now we must mention an often-neglected step:

6. *Urge Your Children to Receive Christ While Young*

Unfortunately, too many Christians think lightly of children's conversions. "They don't un-

derstand what they're doing"; "Their conversions
don't last." Such are the objections we hear. But
we beg to differ. Many children *do* make decisions
which last for life. This author was converted
when he was only eight years old. His wife was
won at ten. Robert Moffat, the great missionary to
Africa, was won when a child. A questionnaire,
asking 1,500 ministers the ages of their conversions, revealed that the average was 12 years.
Yes, children often know what they are doing.
Either the Lord or the Devil gets them when they
are young. Who will get your children?

Mrs. J. G. Kruger, of Canada, who is a mother
and a grandmother, believes in early conversions.
And she puts it into practice in her own family.
Here are her words:

Is there a greater tragedy, a greater sorrow in this
world, than to have grown up sons and daughters *still
without Christ?* Every prayer group receives heart-
breaking requests like the one before me: "Please pray
for the salvation of my three grown-up sons!" Being a
mother, I can understand such grief. But in all love and
the greatest tenderness I must say, "Mother, maybe
ignorantly, you made the greatest mistake ever a
mother could make! You failed to do what the mothers
of Salem did. You failed to *lead* your children to Christ
when they were small." Jesus said, "Suffer the little
children to come unto me, and forbid them not; for of
such is the kingdom of God" (Mark 10:14). We definite-
ly "forbid," keep them back, if we do not give them the
opportunity to decide for Christ.

Mothers, and fathers also, there is no reason why a
child five to eight years old is not a Christian. I love
children and in years of Child Evangelism and in my

own family I have found that there is hardly a child that will not receive Christ if his lost condition is explained to him with the simple way of salvation.

Neither is there any reason when we trust God why the child who is taught, as in Deut. 6:7, should backslide. "And thou shalt teach them diligently unto thy children, and shalt talk of them when thou sittest in thine house, and when thou walkest by the way, and when thou liest down, and when thou risest up." God's Word says, "Train up a child in the way he should go: And when he is old he will not depart from it" (Proverbs 22:6). That is God's Word, and I have found Him true to His Word, although years ago I never realized the ease with which younger children could be led to Christ.

Fear and terror of my own children being lost gripped my heart and led me to bring each child to Him who said, "Suffer the little children to come unto me." I was told, "Yes, they are saved now, but they will backslide." Again with fear and trembling, I cried, "O God, I will trust Thee to keep them, while I, with Thy help do my best to train them according to Thy Word." Oh how wonderfully God has honored my little faith! They did not backslide, but are now happy in His service or preparing for it. Two are now missionaries in Africa.

I led my four-and-one-half-year-old grandson to Christ. He was a difficult child to manage. Now, two weeks later, after a struggle when he had to give in to his mother, he was sulking. Lovingly I whispered, "Would it make Jesus happy if you would go and say, 'I am sorry, Mommy, forgive me?' " Immediately he said, "Yes," ran to the kitchen stretching out his little arms as mother stopped. Then he said, hugging her, "I am sorry, Mommy." Never had he done anything like that before. Oh, the power of God unto salvation in these little hearts!

Many parents wonder: when is the age of accountability? In other words, when does God see a child pass from so-called "innocence" to responsibility for his acceptance or rejection of Jesus Christ?

No one answer can be given. Some believe the age of 12, others five or seven. However, the safest rule is considering the individual personality of your child. Just as I.Q.'s differ, and educators take this into consideration in teaching your child, so you must know the "spiritual I.Q." of your child. Some children, who have had more intensive religious training and atmosphere (minister's children, for example), feel the guilt of sin earlier than do some other youngsters. Study your child, see his reactions when the Gospel is preached. If he seems convicted by the Holy Spirit, by all means offer to pray with him. He will be eternally grateful to you if you do.

"I would have come to the Lord even earlier in life," says a young Christian man, "if someone would have only asked me to come. But I guess they thought that because my father was a minister, I was a Christian too. But I knew that I was not saved. At last I decided to come to God on my own...."

This young man is now an evangelist. And when he ministers in a church, he's quick to ask the minister's and deacon's children if they have been "born again."

"This action naturally hurts some of the parents' pride," he smiles. "Most of them think their children are angels and that they are all right spiritually. When I told a deacon and his wife that I had just led their 11-year-old son to the Lord, they snorted: 'Oh, he's always been a Christian!' But I told them that Donny had told me that he wasn't converted and that he was terribly convicted of his sin. That's why I prayed with him. Of course they were surprised."

Remember, being born and reared in a Christian home does not make your child a Christian. Being born in a barn does not make a person a horse! Each child must make a definite acceptance of Jesus Christ if you want to see each one of them in heaven. Are you sure that your children are born again according to the third chapter of the Gospel of John?

Decide now to make sure that your children receive Christ while they are young. Tomorrow may be too late!

Still another step in leading your children to Christ is:

7. *Don't Be Overly Strict; Allow Some Freedom*

Gordon came from a very strict home. His Christian parents had a religion of "don'ts." No matter what he wanted to do, (and some of his desires weren't wrong), his parents would find some religious reason why he should not do what he wanted. After about 16 years of living in this negative attitude, he left home to go to work on his own. And the first night he was away from home, he became dead drunk!

A long-faced, negative religion causes a young

person's heart to rebel. Sooner or later, he will try
to kick over the traces and enjoy life in a wrong
way.

You cannot expect children to be adults. Boys
will be boys and girls will be girls. Some things
that they will want to do may not appeal to you,
but if the Bible does not forbid these activities,
think over their request. Christianity is full of
man-made traditions, and perhaps your decisions
are made because of these traditions rather than
because of what God says.

Take sports for instance. Many a Christian parent forbids his child to go to a ball game or a
basketball tournament, or some other clean sport,
because these games do not appeal to the parent.
And because the parents frown on such activities,
it is easy for them to feel that God frowns on them
too. Such may not be the case, unless of course the
game is played on the Lord's Day or gambling and
betting is woven into the sport.

Johnny is told, "You can't go. That's no place for
a Christian to be." What's Johnny to do instead?
Gossip on the telephone like his "Christian"
mother does, or overeat at supper time like his
"Christian" father does. Both of these "adult"
habits: gossiping and intemperance are condemned in the Bible. Baseball isn't even mentioned. No wonder Johnny is confused. No wonder
he dreams through his tears of the day when he
will do just what he likes.

What is the solution to this problem? We must
have rules. There are some activities in which
parents must not let their children engage: cheat-

ing, stealing, lying, and other sins condemned by the Bible. But other activities: sports, parties, hikes, listening to the radio or watching television, playing records, etc. must be dealt with in a spirit of love and broadmindedness. To condemn *all* sports, *all* broadcasts, *all* telecasts is being "too strict."

None of these things are wrong in themselves. However, if certain telecasts or sports violate Bible principles, then these individual matters must be condemned. But don't make broad generalizations.

If you condemn everything except church, Sunday school, and prayer meetings, you will likely lose your child's soul. He needs these activities, but he needs fun, fellowship, and exercise as well. Don't try to make your child an old, settled adult. Give him some freedom and you will have greater success in leading him to Christ.

Closely related to this point is another key to your children's souls:

8. *Keep Them Busy in Constructive, Christian Activities*

The old saying "Satan finds work for idle hands to do," is all too true. But it's also a fact that "Christ will give work for willing hands to do."

Many Christian parents need to learn to accentuate the positive. Make Christianity a life of "do's" rather than "don'ts" and your children will love it.

Here's an example. If you do not want Johnny to

go to a questionable amusement place, tell him that you have something better and more exciting planned. Maybe it will be a nature hike, a time when you will show him some of God's handiwork. Or how about a tract-distributing contest downtown? See who can give out the most tracts, Johnny or Dad. In other words, balance your negative command with some positive action. Children love activity. They are alive with boundless energy. Why not channel this into Christian service? Your children will *want to* come to Christ.

Still another vital factor is:

9. *Be Aware of Your Children's Habits*

Once habits are formed, they make it more difficult for people to believe that they can live the Christian life. If your children pick up the undesirable habits, swearing, smoking, lying, cheating, and others, nip these habits in the bud.

A Christian father told a minister recently: "Before I knew it, my son had picked up the smoking habit. By the time I was ready to help him overcome it, I found that it had a mighty hold on his life. He told me he couldn't break it.... Today, he's a successful businessman, but he thinks he can't become a Christian until he can break the nicotine power. Oh, if I only would have nipped it before it got such a stranglehold on him...."

It's true that Christ can break the strongest habit. But sometimes it's hard to convince the sinner of this fact. Play it safe by dealing with these habits as they arise. Show your children how these habits can lead to cancer, theft, and other tragic dead-end streets. A good "scare-talk" sometimes helps. Other times, love and patience does more good.

Ask God for wisdom in discovering your children's easily-picked-up habits. Pray for strength to deal with them in a firm but Christlike manner. This will help you win your children to Christ.

An overlooked point in family soul-winning is this:

10. Be Careful of the Vicinity in Which You Live

There is a saying, "God made the country but man made the city to run around in."

Whether you rear your children in the country or the city, be careful to select a good environment for your children.

Lot chose Sodom to live in purely from a materialistic viewpoint. Morally and spiritually Sodom was the worst place he could have chosen. But like many Christian parents, he thought "business is business." As a result, his daughters did evil and his longing-for-Sodom wife became a pillar of salt. He should have thought of this ungodly environment before he "took a job" in that wicked city.

Joubert has widely observed: "We are all of us more or less echoes, repeating involuntarily the virtues, the defects, the movements and characters of those among whom we live."

Before you decide to move to a new community because of material gain, ask yourself: will this mean spiritual loss to my family? Remember, "the steps of a good man are ordered of the Lord" and so are "the stops." Should you move or stay put? The Lord will tell you if you really want to know His will.

Another point that goes hand-in-hand with this:

11. Be Mindful of Your Children's Friends

These are truth-packed words: "A man is known by the company he keeps. He's also known by the company he doesn't keep."

As a parent, you have the right to choose the proper clothes, the best food, and the right places for your children to attend. It is also your responsibility to allow your children to play with good friends and to forbid them to associate with evil playmates.

Remember, some children are morally and spiritually poison to your children. These "sin-carriers" will teach your youngsters to steal, lie, smoke, and engage in immoral habits. The "gang instinct" may cause your children to commit evil deeds—through social pressure—that they would never think of doing by themselves.

So help them choose friends who are clean, honest, and Sunday school attendants. Their influence will help you in the big task of leading your children to Christ.

And when these youngsters become teenagers and aim their sights for higher education, help them.

12. Choose the Best College

Not just the best academically but the best for them spiritually. This does not mean that they must attend a Christian college (although this is considered best by many religious leaders). But it does mean that you must feel that their Christian training will flourish, not diminish, during these very formative years.

A secular college may be best for your "genius" if you are sure that he is well-established in his faith and well-able to refute the damnable doctrines of evolution and much so-called "science." But if Johnny has had a hard time being a Christian in high school, think twice before you put him in an agnostic atmosphere of a secular college.

A young man told Dr. Bob Jones, Sr., how he had been reared in a Christian home, how he had gone to a secular college, had lost his faith in the Bible, had become loose morally, and now was thinking of suicide because his body was full of venereal disease. No education is worth this price!

Guard your teenager by wise guidance to higher education. The college he attends may determine his eternal destiny.

And then, remember, someday your grown-up children will be making plans about walking down the aisle with the ones they have chosen for life. At this time, you can give them knowledge gained through years of experience. And if you give it in a helpful, non-dogmatic manner, your children will thank you for it.

Therefore, guide them as they

13. Choose a Life Partner

What does this have to do with winning your child to Christ? Well, in the majority of cases, if your child's wife or husband is not a "born-again" believer, he or she will lead your child far from the way of God. It is of paramount importance that your son or daughter marry a believer. You must do all within your power to encourage your own flesh and blood to choose only Christian "dates." Kindly but firmly discourage going with unbelievers. The Bible frowns on "the unequal yoke." So you have God backing you in your convictions.

However, if your son or daughter will not receive your advice, then commit the matter to the Lord. And should they marry unsaved individuals, accept those they have chosen. Show a Christ-like attitude. Then focus your prayers on both of them until they come to Christ.

And now a final word in winning your children to Christ.

14. Refuse to Be Defeated

Remember, "delays do not mean denials." Days, months, and years may pass before your children are won to Christ. But don't be impatient. God is never in a hurry but He's always on time. He hears your prayers. He is dealing with your children's hearts. So don't be discouraged. God is still on the throne. He can soften the hardest heart. Don't give in to discouragement, the devil's best tool. Don't let him use it on you.

George Mueller, the giant of faith, prayed daily for the salvation of two men. Even on his deathbed, Mr. Mueller believed that God would answer his prayers and save these men. A short time after his death, a mighty revival swept that part of England. Both of these men were genuinely converted!

For years, a gray-haired mother prayed for the salvation of her daughter, Edith Mae Pennington, a beautiful school-teacher. When her daughter won a beauty contest and Hollywood offered Edith Mae a contract, the mother announced: "If you go to Hollywood against my wishes, Edith Mae, I'm going with you—to pray for you until you turn to the Lord."

Strong-willed Edith Mae went to Hollywood. And so did her mother. While the young beauty was busy acting and getting 50 dollars for every "posed" smile, her mother was in the room at the back of the stage—praying for her prodigal daughter.

"Finally, I couldn't stand it any longer," Edith Mae confesses. "God answered my mother's prayers by convicting me of my sins and self-seeking. I became very miserable. I remained in that unhappy condition until I repented to the Lord. Now I am saved and happy—serving Him!"

God, who answered Mother Pennington's prayers, will answer yours. He will help you win your children to Himself. Trust Him for His help—TODAY.

Then you can answer in the affirmative the question this poem asks:

ARE ALL THE CHILDREN IN?

I think ofttimes as the night draws nigh
Of an old house on the hill,
Of a yard all wide and blossom-starred
Where the children played at will.
And when the night at last came down,
Hushing the merry din,
Mother would look around and ask,
"Are all the children in?"

'Tis many and many a year since then,
And the old house on the hill
No longer echoes to childish feet,
And the yard is still, so still.
But I see it all, as the shadows creep,
And though many the years have been
Since then, I can hear mother ask,
"Are all the children in?"

I wonder if when the shadows fall
On the last short, earthly day,
When we say goodbye to the world outside,
All tired with our childish play,
When we step out into that Other Land
Where mother so long has been,
Will we hear her ask, just as of old,
"Are all the children in?"

Chapter Three
Your Wife Can Be Won

Chapter Three

A few years ago a prominent manufacturer in an Eastern state became a Christian. He then determined to try to win his pretty brunette wife to the Lord.

It wasn't easy. "Church! Church! Church! Can't you ever go anywhere else?" she nagged. "You seem to think of no one but God anymore!"

She threatened to leave him. But he suggested, "Let's take a vacation in California. I'm sure we can work out our difficulties, honey."

A change of climate didn't seem to help. "Believe what you will, I personally don't believe there is a God!" she boldly blurted. Heartsick at his wife's attitude, the manufacturer prayed desperately that the Holy Spirit would convict her and draw her to the Lord.

Soon prayer was answered. One night, while

driving down the coast of California, his wife moved over closer to him and whispered: "Honey, I really didn't mean what I said about God. I really believe in Him and I want Him in my life, too."

"Thank God!" the husband smiled. "He has answered my prayers."

That night around 11 o'clock they found a small church open. They walked in, went to the altar, and soon the joy of salvation flooded the wife's heart, too.

Today, this Christian manufacturer, now the father of five children, would gladly tell you, "Yes, a husband can win his wife to Christ. God still answers prayer."

Perhaps the greatest factor in winning your wife to Christ is this:

1. Love Her

"Oh, she knows I love her or else I wouldn't have married her," many a husband says in defense. "Why do I have to tell her?"

Simply because a woman loves to be told that she is loved. She does not like to be taken for granted. So if you want to win her, remember that the most important objective she lives for is to love and be loved. Sincerely tell her at least once a day that you love her or think she's pretty or that you're glad you married her. Remember, a wife isn't preached to Christ, criticized to God or argued to Christianity. She must be *loved* to Christ. And this is where you, as her Christian husband, hold the main key to her salvation.

Dr. Oswald J. Smith points out that "there are two kinds of wives. There are those who love to demonstrate their affection. They meet you at the door, throw their arms around you and give you a welcoming kiss. They go to you of their own accord and crawl into your arms. If there is anything between you they make it up at once. They are just like a clinging vine and they are priceless. They know just how to make you love them and to make you happy.

"Then there is the other kind. They are reserved. You have to take the initiative. They may love you more deeply than the first and they will express their affection for you in their letters. But they do not show it when they are with you. If there are any misunderstandings they just suffer and wait until *you* make up. Their love is true but undemonstrative. You will have to go more than halfway if you want to be happy. They have much to give, but they do not know how to give it, and you must teach them. You must win them. You must go the second mile. They may even resist you. Their response may be disappointing. But it will pay you to persevere."

Yes, only as you persevere in love, can you hope to win your wife to Christ.

Gordon L. Van Oostenburg comments in his excellent tract "Marriage Can Be Happy" (courtesy American Tract Society, Oradell, New Jersey):

God's pattern for the happy marriage as revealed through His truth is "love." Without it marriage cannot succeed. With it, despite the lack of material advantages, marriage can be as God designed it. How many couples begin married life with the attitude that their mate must make them happy and that it is the mate's duty to do so. They enter holy wedlock looking for something rather than with the intention of giving themselves to one another. "Submitting yourselves one to another in the fear of God," we read in Ephesians 5:21. This is the Lord's way. People who enter marriage with the attitude of getting instead of giving are quick to find fault with one another. Little things irritate and disturb them, such as personal habits, ways of speaking, and mannerisms. These lead to quarrels and tension mounts while the divine pattern of "love" is ignored....

God speaks of this love in I Corinthians 13. It is only possible to the person who in repentance to God and faith in Jesus Christ has become a new person. This love of Christ must be applied in our relations with each other. How convicting these words are to the self-centered self-willed person. Listen as God says "... love suffereth long, and is kind; love envieth not; ... seeketh not her own, is not easily provoked, thinketh no evil; ... Beareth all things, believeth all things, hopeth all things, endureth all things. Love never faileth" (see I Corinthians 13:4-8). When you feel neglected, feel that you have been overlooked, or ignored, it only reveals your lack of love. When you are so easily upset and disturbed about your partner's mannerisms it only reveals your lack of love. When you become suspicious and think evil of your mate, it only reveals your lack of love. When you feel you have gone far enough and you are ready to quit, it only shows your lack of love. "Love never faileth." This is the secret. Love so that you expect nothing from your ... wife, but go all out to please your partner, making it your aim to make her ... happy. It is the only pattern for a Christian marriage.

2. Pray For Her

Spend more time talking to God about your wife than you do talking to your wife about God. It isn't how many words you say that counts; it's how power-packed they are that really matters. So pray, pray, pray.

Don't be afraid or ashamed to let your wife hear you praying for her. It may make her angry at the time, and she may tell you, "What do you think I am? A Heathen?" But don't worry. It will touch her heart to hear you say her name in prayer.

A Christian singer tells how he prayed and prayed for his wife's conversion. But the more he prayed the worse she seemed to become. She persecuted him, treated him shamefully, and did everything she could to discourage him. However, he kept a kind, loving attitude toward her. He continued praying and believing. Finally, her stubborn will broke, and she received Christ into her heart, too. Today, they are evangelistic singers, thanks to God and the prayer and perseverance of her husband. He admits that it wasn't easy but it was certainly worthwhile. A soul was won!

Before we go on to the third step in winning your wife, remember these words of I Peter 3:7: "Likewise, ye husbands, dwell with them according to knowledge (live considerately with your wives), giving honor unto the wife, as unto the weaker vessel, and as being heirs together of the grace of life *that your prayers be not hindered.*"

3. Give Her Sincere Compliments

There is a saying, "More people die of a broken heart than of a swelled head." Unfortunately, many a husband forgets to compliment his wife and then he wonders why her affection for him dies.

The Bible says: "Her children arise up and call her blessed; her husband also, and *he praiseth her*" (Proverbs 31:28). Yes, a husband should praise or compliment his wife. Everyone wants to be appreciated. Praise your wife when she makes your favorite dish, when she is helpful and understanding, when she wears a dress you especially like. Make it a habit to look for something to compliment her about. You will be surprised to see that this will soften her heart and make her easier to win to Christ.

4. *Appeal to Her Social Nature*

Most women are very sociable. They like parties, shopping sprees, and telephone chats.

You can use this trait to help you in winning your wife to the Lord. Find a couple of Christian women where you worship who have personalities which would appeal to your wife. Perhaps they may have something in common with your wife—such as a love for plants, sewing or knitting. Encourage them to make friends with your wife (without letting on that you tipped them off, of course). Their friendships and invitations may win your wife. A woman knows how to win a woman. They talk the same language!

5. *Lead Your Family in Family Altar*

Most wives, even though they do not want to pay the price of being a Christian themselves, want their children to turn out well. If you can convince your wife that a family altar will benefit your children, she will be interested.

Joshua declared, "As for me and my house we will serve the Lord" (Joshua 24:15). It's up to you, sir, to lead in family worship. And as you do, weave in powerful Gospel passages from the New Testament. Thus your wife will hear God's simple plan of salvation. This will help you in winning her to the Savior.

6. *Take Your Children to Sunday School*

What they learn they repeat. Soon your wife will be getting the Gospel from the lips of those darlings she loves, your children. Many a wife has been drawn to Christ through the witness of her own "flesh and blood." (See chapter 4 for more details.)

7. *Make the Most of Her Emotional Experiences*

A mother told me, "If it had not been for the tragic car accident that killed our son, I doubt that I would be a Christian today."

Many a wife has come to Christ in an hour of sickness or sorrow. When the heart is broken, Gospel seed enters more easily.

When sickness or sorrow strikes your family, be ready to comfort your wife with the fact that we have a wonderful Friend in Jesus. In her sorrow, she may seek the Lord.

There are many other ways you can win your wife to Jesus: through women-slanted Christian magazines and books *(Angel Unawares, A Man Called Peter,* and *The Burden is Light);* by select Gospel broadcasts with story appeal—such as "Unshackled!" and the testimonies of such women as Colleen Townsend, Dale Evans, Eugenia Price, and others.

One negative commandment in closing: don't make her habits or apparel an issue. Many wives see only the things they will have to give up if they become a Christian. Make only one thing important in her mind: her receiving or rejecting Jesus Christ. If she receives Christ, He will convict her of her sinful habits and worldly dress. Let God do His part. You concentrate on your part: lead her to Christ.

Through prayer, consecrated psychology, and perserverance, your wife can be won!

Chapter Four
Your Parents Can Be Won

Chapter Four

A little girl pleaded with her agnostic father. "Please come to church with me, just once. I love you, Daddy. Won't you please come?"

Finally he said, "Okay, honey, just once."

His little daughter was overjoyed. She loved Jesus and now she hoped her father would hear a sermon that would make him love the Lord, too.

But she was terribly disappointed. Her pastor read a lengthy Old Testament passage that was full of long, difficult names. Nearly every verse said, "So and so begat so and so and then he died ... then he died ... then he died."

"Oh, Daddy will never want to come to church again," she sobbed to her mother.

But she was wrong. God used that phrase "and he died" to convict and convert her father. He testified later that those three words haunted him for days afterwards. He realized that some day he would die unprepared. At last he decided to make his peace with God. His little daughter had led him to Christ.

Lydia H. Sigourney says: "We speak of educating our children. Do we know that our children also educate us?"

Yes, children can win their parents to Christ by following these principles:

1. Living Obediently and Lovingly At Home

An unsaved father said, in reference to his "Christian" daughter who has an ugly disposition, "If that's a Christian, I don't want to be one!"

If you want to win your parents to Christ, you must live the Christian life daily at home. Otherwise your parents will say, "Your actions speak so loud that I can't hear what you're saying."

You must be obedient. The fifth commandment says: "Honor thy father and mother" (Exodus 20:12). So long as you do not violate your Christian principles by doing what your unsaved parents tell you, be obedient to them. This is a vital step in leading them to Christ.

You must be loving. Your parents have their faults, but you have some, too. Love them in spite of their faults. Test every word, every action by this question: "Did I do that in love?" There's no place in your life as a Christian for "sassing back," for sarcasm, for temper tantrums. Remember, you're representing a God of love. So act like it.

2. Prayer and Witnessing

Pray for opportunities to speak a word for Christ to your parents. Read II Kings 5:1-14. See how the little maid in Naaman's house gave the right word at the right time and how her simple statement resulted in her master seeking God's servant, Elisha. Finally, Naaman was cured of his leprosy.

When your parents mention the sudden death of a person, you can comment: "Yes, the Bible says, 'It is appointed unto man once to die and after this the judgment' " (Hebrews 9:27). When friends fail, mention that Jesus never fails. Use wisdom and ask God to guide you in saying the right word at the right time.

3. Taking a Kind But Firm Non-compromising Stand

If your parents see that your faith is something you really live for and will even die for, they will be interested in your beliefs. But if you can violate Christian principles when it suits you, they will sneeringly retort: "Sweep your own doorstep before you look for dirt on mine."

My father, Peter Olson, made up his mind that he would not compromise in his home. This was not an easy decision to make. His parents and brothers and sisters were unsaved. Often the Swedes would gather on Saturday evenings for an "old time" dance in his parents' home. (Peter used to play for them before his conversion.) But on such occasions, he would go away to find Christian fellowship among other teenagers.

His non-compromise position soon had its influence on his parents. When they returned from the
dance hall, they would see their son's glasses rest-
ing on his Bible, a silent witness that the last
thing he did before retiring was to read God's
Word and pray. This testimony smote their hearts
with conviction. At last Jonas Olson and his wife,
both in their 60s repented of their sins and trusted
the Christ their son served. With tears streaming
down his wrinkled old face, the prodigal father
told his son, "Peter, it's largely because of your life
and firm Christian stand that I'm coming to
Christ today."

Yes, noncompromise pays. So decide today to be
true to Jesus. Live the Christian life. Don't lower
your standards. Kindly but firmly take your stand
for the things of God. And the Lord will honor
your faithfulness by giving you the souls of your
parents.

4. Inviting Parents to Gospel Services

Perhaps you have sung, "Bring them in; bring
them in from the fields of sin." By your invitation,
given in love, you may bring your parents in from
the fields of sin. Invite them to your Sunday
school (Mother's and Father's Days are ideal
times to invite your parents), ask them to come to
see you graduate from the Vacation Bible School
you have been attending. Youth for Christ rallies,
Christian banquets, Singspirations, and other
Christian endeavors are there to serve you and
your parents. "Use all means to win some." Surely

one of these places will appeal to your parents. So invite them. The worst they can say is "No." But they may say "Yes, we'll go."

The Christmas concert or Easter program at your church is a big attraction to most parents. Many people get religious at least twice a year: Christmas and Easter. Therefore these times are perfect for you to throw out the Gospel net. Perhaps you'll make a catch—two souls!

Remember, your parents are interested in YOU. So when you've been asked to sing, say a poem, play an instrument, or any other form of service of a public nature, ask your parents to come and hear you. Most likely they will. Therefore, do your very best so that they will be impressed by what Jesus means in your life and work.

The power of personal invitation and parental interest in their children is shown in this letter written by Mrs. Dave Peters (Idee Peters) of California. She writes:

Like most new converts, I thought the members of my family would be eager to be saved too when they heard about my conversion. I discovered, however, that even though they were glad that I was serving the Lord, they were not ready to surrender their own lives to Him. Many, many times I invited them to church and quite often they went with me, usually just to hear me sing. I can still see the look of conviction in their eyes as I sang such songs as "That One Lost Sheep" and "Now I Belong To Jesus." But they just didn't seem to want to come out and out for God.

The one thing God used in winning my loved ones

was my ministry in song. They would sometimes accuse me of preaching to them at home. But they always accepted and enjoyed my singing ministry without a word of criticism.

In 1959, 13 years after my conversion, I was invited to sing for revival meetings in Pennsylvania, 15 miles from my home town. I was thrilled! I flew from warm California to 20-degree eastern weather. My arrival was a complete surprise to my family. But each night, Mother and Father drove me to the meetings. (Dad would invite others to come and hear his daughter, Idee, sing.)

One song entitled, "I'll Never Be Lonely Again" I was requested to sing again and again. It seemed to be the one song God especially blessed during these meetings. It helped break the strong will of my parents so that they both came to Christ during the first week of services. Other conversions that first week were: two sisters, an uncle, twin nephews, a twin niece and nephew, and three other relatives. There were 40 decisions in the first week; 100 in three weeks. And many of them testified that this song had helped them make their decision. My sister wrote me recently, "I'll always love that song. You sang it the night I got saved." Yes, I'm glad that I invited my parents to hear me sing because God used it to help bring their souls to Himself.

Your invitation, song, word, or whatever talent the Lord has given you can help bring your parents to a personal knowledge of Jesus Christ. Do your part and God will do His.

If you no longer live at home—perhaps you live hundreds of miles from your parents—we suggest you follow these practical pointers:

First, be faithful in writing to your parents regularly. Their hearts long to hear from you. Don't disappoint them. A busy radio preacher makes it a rule to write his parents once a week. You can, too. There's a warm, personal touch about a letter which, if consecrated to the Lord, can be used in soul-winning. One lady (an invalid) has had over 1,500 people receive Christ as a result of her loving, Gospel-seasoned letters. Don't make your letters "preachy." Just skillfully weave in one or two appropriate Scriptures in each letter along with a personal testimony of what Christ means to you. Your parents will read the Gospel according to *you*.

Second, if you hear of an evangelistic crusade in your parents' city, urge them to attend. Or invite them to listen to the good music you enjoy on such-and-such a broadcast, or to watch a minister you think presents the Gospel interestingly on television. No doubt they will follow your suggestion and thereby hear the Word of God. So follow your suggestion with much prayer.

Third, invite your parents to your home for a visit. Let them see you enjoy a family altar. Let them watch a Christian family in action, putting the Bible into everyday life. Invite them to attend Sunday school and church with you. And if the sermon strikes home, offer to go to the altar with them. They can find salvation during their vacation.

After his wife's death, Grandpa Woolsey stayed with his daughter, Olive, and her husband, a minister of the Gospel. Little by little the white-haired grandfather, now in his 80's, *saw* what real

faith in Christ did for his daughter and family.
One night, he raised his hand during the invitation time and humbly came forward to receive
Christ. By having her father in her home, Olive
helped win him to the Lord.

Fourth, encourage other Christians, ministers,
or laymen, to visit your parents. Most older people
get very lonely and therefore doubly appreciate a
visit. A card or letter to a minister or Christian
friend where your parents live may result in visits
which may help win your parents to God.

Marie was greatly burdened for her aged father
who lay in the hospital at Yorkton, Saskatche-
wan, Canada. But how could she help him? She
lived 1500 miles away in British Columbia. She
didn't have the fare for such a long trip.

At last she got an idea. She would write a letter
to a minister in Yorkton, urging him to visit her
unsaved father. So she addressed the envelope to:
The *(a certain denomination)* Minister, Yorkton,
Sask. It reached him. But due to his busy
schedule, he was unable to visit her father right
away. In desperation, Marie wrote another letter,
then sent a telegram. The latter communication
aroused action. The minister and his wife visited
Marie's father, Tom Wilson, and told him how his
daughter had requested that they see him. He was
very pleased. And when they told him of Marie's
concern for his soul, he broke down and prayed the
penitent's prayer. Another father had been converted because of his daughter's concern and a
minister's visit.

Friend, follow these practical suggestions. Pray

much. Look for every opportunity you can to reach your parents with the "greatest story ever told." And I'm sure God will reward your efforts by convicting and converting the dearest on earth to you—your mother and father!

Chapter Five
Others
Can Be Won

Chapter Five

To help you lead others of your relatives and friends to Christ, we offer you the following effective plan for leading someone to Christ.

1. Show Him His Need of Salvation

"By one man sin entered into the world, and death by sin; and so death passed upon all men, for that all have sinned" (Romans 5:12). "The soul that sinneth, it shall die" (Ezek. 18:4).

2. Show Him That His Only Hope of Salvation Is In Christ and His Finished Work

"For there is none other Name under heaven given among men, whereby we must be saved" (Acts 4:12). "Christ came into the world to save sinners" (I Tim. 1:15). "Whosoever will may come"

(Rev. 22:17). "All we like sheep have gone astray; we have turned every one to his own way; and the Lord hath laid on Him the iniquity of us all" (Isa. 53:6; See also John 5:24, and I Peter 2:24).

3. Show Him How Salvation In Christ Is Obtained

By repentance (Luke 13:3; Acts 2:38), confession (Romans 10:9), and appropriating faith (Acts 2:38; Romans 10:9; John 3:16; Acts 10:43; Acts 16:31).

"If thou shalt confess with thy mouth the Lord Jesus, and shalt believe in thine heart that God hath raised Him from the dead, thou shalt be saved" (Romans 10:9).

4. Show Him That He Who Is Able to Save Is Able to Keep

"Fear thou not; for I am with thee: be not dismayed; for I am thy God: I will strengthen thee; yea, I will help thee; yea, I will uphold thee with the right hand of My righteousness" (Isa. 41:10).

Moreover, point out to him the necessity of watchfulness and prayer (Mark 14:38; Col. 4:2); of daily studying the Word (2 Tim. 2:15; also 3:14-17; Josh. 1:8); of witnessing for Christ (Isa. 43:10); and of a life of soul-winning service (Dan. 12:3).

Texts to Cover Special Cases

The following objections are among those most frequently met with in dealing with the unsaved.

The texts of Scripture indicated, as well as similar passages, may be used in such cases.

1. "Not today," or "Some other time." 2 Cor. 6:2; Heb. 2:3; Heb. 3:15.

2. "Don't feel like it." Isa. 55:6 and 7; Acts 17:30 and 31.

3. "Am too great a sinner." Isa. 1:18; Matt. 9:13; I Tim. 1:15.

4. "Am good enough now," or "Am satisfied with my present experience." Rom. 6:23; Gal. 3:10; James 2:10.

5. "Too many hypocrites in the church." John 21:22; Rom. 14:12.

6. "Couldn't hold out." I Cor. 10:13; I Peter 1:5; Jude 24.

Realizing the need for some inspiration, we close this book with some excellent suggestions on soul-winning.

Soul-winning is a task and a privilege from which no Christian is exempt. All are commissioned, "Go ye ... and preach the Gospel" (Mark 16:15).

Christ is depending upon us. He has limited Himself to work through human channels. "You shall be witnesses unto Me," said our ascending Lord, as He assigned us our supreme earthly task. (Acts 1:8).

Witnessing for Christ is the greatest work in the world. It is the most honoring to Christ, the most joyful to the Christian, and the most beneficial in its blessed effects to those who are won.

To agree with your Lord—that you will consistently witness—is the first step. Then your motto for future days will be "I am willing to do my best." He cannot ask any more of you, and in intimate fellowship with Christ, you will hear Him say, "I will make you to become a fisher of men."

The accompanying sketch will make clear the necessary elements in personal witnessing and soul winning.

This is a divine work through human instruments. Therefore, there will be the spiritual side to it as well as the natural.

The Need of Consecration

We began with the need of consecration. This is the starting point. Without a real, vital and living experience with Christ each day there will not be a grip in our witness.

"Abide in Me" (John 15:4), He says. Make My heart your home. My blood your refuge for cleansing. My wisdom, My power, My joy, My life, your sufficiency.

Though we speak with the tongues of men and of angels and have not love—a rich love for Christ and a love for those He loves—our witness will be as sounding brass and a tinkling cymbal. (I Cor. 13). Those to whom we speak or whom we are trying in some way to influence will detect our lack, though they may fail to name it.

The Ephesian Church was full of witnessing and working Christians, but there was something wrong and our Lord named it, "Thou didst leave thy first love." "Repent..." He said, "or else I will come ... quickly and remove your candlestick" (Rev. 2:1-5).

"Out of the abundance of the heart the mouth speaketh." If Christ dwells deep down in your heart by faith, we will make much of Him when the opportunity to witness arrives, and the Holy Spirit will see that we have opportunities if He knows that what we are, what we do, and what we say will exalt the Lord Jesus Christ.

Daily Bible reading and prayer promote and maintain the heart fellowship with Christ. Constant, consecutive meditation upon the Scriptures is a necessity.

Look for a fuller view of Christ; the Living Word, in the Written Word. "In the volume of the Book it is written of Me" (Psalm 40:7). Then turn your meditation into prayer, for the power to lift Him up till all men are drawn unto Him. (John 3:14-15; John 12:32.)

The fruit of this companionship with Him will be a growing concern for those around you who are out of Christ. This concern is vital. Without it, all our Christian effort will be mechanical and powerless. It is the concern of Jesus that we need, not our own worked-up concern. The Holy Spirit registers this within us according to our capacity at the moment, spiritually, to feel as Jesus feels about these deluded and desperately needy people all around us.

Meditation upon the following Scriptures, firstly, in the presence of Christ, and then in the company of the unsaved, will give the opportunity to the Spirit of God to make this concern ours:

"He that believeth not the Son shall not see life; but the wrath of God abideth on him" (John 3:36).

"When I say unto the wicked, O wicked man, thou shalt surely die; if thou dost not speak to warn the wicked from his way, that wicked man shall die in his iniquity; but his blood will I require at thine hand" (Ezekiel 33:8).

The saintly William C. Burns, so used by God in Scotland and China, was met by his mother one day in a Glasgow street, and he was "weeping at the sight of the multitudes in the streets, so many of whom are passing through life unsaved," he said.

Sinful Bashfulness

The Lord Jesus said, "I must work the works of Him that sent me, while it is yet day: the night cometh when no man can work" (John 9:4). Surely we feel this divine compulsion. No man will do anything really great until he feels that he must! This is the reason for lingering, in this article, on this matter of an abiding concern for the salvation of others. When this passion, this hidden fire takes hold of your life, you will earnestly seek deliverance from sinful bashfulness, pride, and the common excuses for not doing this work, and the Holy Spirit will hear your cry, meet your need and use your witness.

The Right Contact

Be armed with the best suitable tracts. Know your tracts and never be without some. You may like to put your name and address in each. Follow up with believing prayer every tract or paper handed out, and where possible contact the person again to find out tactfully its effect, and to answer any questions.

Learn the art of spiritual diagnosis. Find out his knowledge of Christ and the Gospel. Get clearly his attitude toward Christ. "What do you think of Christ?" is the big question you must return to repeatedly.

Does he admit his own desperate need of Christ? Use the Scriptures freely. Pray, as you get him to read. Expect the Holy Spirit to apply the Scriptures to his need.

As you sense that the Spirit of God is working, convicting him of his sin, and revealing his need of Christ, ask him, "Will you receive the Lord Jesus Christ as your Saviour and Lord, NOW?"

Don't overpress him. Never encourage anyone to come to Christ halfheartedly. If he responds, ask him to kneel with you. Open your Bible at Isaiah 53:6 and make plain once more what God has done with his sin, and what his sin did to Christ.

Then get him to read John 1:12 and see that he must "receive" Christ, and thank the Lord Jesus for dying for him. Then turn to Revelation 3:20 and show him the wonderful promise:

"Behold, I stand at the door and knock: if any man hear My voice, and open the door, I will come in to him, and will sup with him and he with Me."

Assist him to pray something like this: "Lord Jesus, I believe that Thou art the One who died for me, and paid the full debt of my sin on the cross. I am sorry that I have sinned against Thee. I repent, and I ask Thee to have mercy on me, and to forgive me, and to cleanse me from all unrighteousness.

"I now receive Thee into my life as my Savior and Lord, to take entire charge of my life. And with Thy help, from this moment on, I am determined to live for Thee, and to serve Thee alone. Amen."

Ask him the question "Where is Christ now?" and make sure he believes Christ is within—in accordance with His promise. (Rev. 3:20; John 6:37; Matt. 11:28-30). This is most important.

Give him clear instruction concerning daily Bible reading and prayer, and encourage him to witness immediately. Introduce him to your pastor and to your local Christian fellowship, and continue to stand by him as he advances spiritually, giving deeper advice as he is able to receive it.

Remember, the greatest thing on earth that a Christian can do is to win a soul to Christ, and it's a work that every *real* Christian is doing.

YOUR FAMILY CAN BE WON!